To Zoetta,

May God
continue to bless a
keep you. You
one of my role!
Keep the Faith!
Thanks for your supp

Love
Peggie M. Hall

Fast Forward Faith

"Moving at the speed of FAITH!"

Peggie M. Hall

Martrice Publishing
Saginaw, MI

Martrice Publishing
P.O. Box 14986
Saginaw, MI 48601
Phone: (989) 755-5884

ISBN: 1-892398-02-8

Printed in the United States of America
Lightning Source Printing
1246 Heil Quaker Blvd
Lavergne, Tennessee 37086

This book is printed on acid-free paper.

Introduction

Source:

"Now faith is the substance of things hoped for, the evidence of things not seen."
~ Hebrews 11:1 ~

By FAITH...

- The Elders obtained a good report
- The world was framed by the Word of God
- Abel offered unto God a more excellent sacrifice than Cain
- Abel, being dead yet, speaks from the ground
- The invisible becomes visible
- Enoch was translated that he should not see death
- Enoch's testimony pleased God
- Diligent seekers are rewarded
- Noah moved to prepare an ark and save his household
- Noah became an heir of righteousness
- Abraham went out to an unknown place
- Abraham received his inheritance
- Abraham sojourned into the land of promise
- Abraham offered up his son Isaac as a sacrifice (God intervened)
- Isaac blessed Jacob and Esau concerning things to come
- Jacob, when he was dying, blessed both of Joseph's sons
- Joseph made mention of the departing of the children of Israel
- Moses, when he was born, was hidden for three months from his parents, because they saw he was a proper child
- Moses refused to be called the son of Pharaoh's daughter
- Moses refused to enjoy the pleasures of sin for a season
- Moses forsook Egypt, not fearing the wrath of the king
- Moses kept the Passover and the sprinkling of blood
- The children of Israel passed through the Red Sea on dry land
- The walls of Jericho fell down
- Rahab was spared
- Kingdoms are subdued
- Righteousness is wrought
- Promises are obtained – needs are met

- The mouth of lions are stopped
- Violent fires lose their heat
- Men are made strong in weakness
- Men achieve Victory…and Deliverance comes
- Dead are raised

Acknowledgements

To God be the Glory for everything I have the strength and the wisdom to do.

To the editors, Jennifer Dexter, Ramona Allen, and my friends and sisters in Christ, Gina Osborne and Ruby Jackson, I say "thank you" for your continued support and encouragement.

To all my co-workers, thank you for allowing me to share my faith with you on a daily basis. I am grateful for your strength and perseverance.

I am fortunate to have the love and support of my loving husband, Gary, and my awesome God-loving, God-fearing daughters, Ramona and Tifani.

To my special son, Toriano Sr., you are a blessing to me. God has granted me a precious gift, my grandson, Toriano, Jr. May his heritage of FAITH exceed every preceding generation, and may God grant each generation to come , even greater FAITH.

Finally, to my father, the wisest man I know. Your support, love, and FAITH have been a guiding light on my darkest days. Keep the FAITH; it's working for you. Thank you for who you are, and for all you have done to assist me in my FAITH walk.

This book is also dedicated to my little brother, Lilton Howard.

Dedication

This book is dedicated to the many women in my life that have demonstrated great FAITH…and to the many other beautiful women of faith that I love so dearly. I will always remember the lessons of FAITH they taught by example.

To the memory of my grandmothers, Marriah Howard and Alice Jones, and my aunt Fannie L. Buchanan…

To my mother, Dasie Lee Howard…

To Ramona Allen and Tifani Hall -- my daughters…

To Jada, Jasmine, Asia, and Kiara -- my god-daughters…

To Annie Love, Dasie Howard, Loretta Jackson, Judy Moore, Elaine Straughter, and Valerie Gardner – my beautiful sisters…

To my special sisters, Florence Hall, Jerry Hall, Tina Hall, and Nancy Smith…

To Donya Buchanan – my special child…

To Sadie Mae Simpson, Alice Holliday, Sarah Dobson, Minnie Franks, Ida Gordon, Beauty Holliday, and Annie S. Jones – my special aunties…

To my special mother-in-law, Mary Hall…

To a special group of sister-girlfriends in my life: Earleen Smithers, Barbara Sane, Gina Osborne, Quencie Neely, Lera Aikin, Marlyn Reeves, Cheryl Smith, LaCreta Clark, Beatrice Manning, Thelma Williams, Faye Hardrick, Sara Jones, Kathreen O'Daniel, Patricia Williams, Lametria Johnson-Eaddy, Winnie Crawford, Emma Ruth Edwards, and Shirley Rice…

To my lifelong friend and cousin, Virgie M. Kendricks…

To Priscilla Nicholas, Minnie Buchanan...

In memory of Verdia Nickson-Price

To the precious memory of Mrs. Mary Alice Scott and Hurlette Coleman-Dickens, women of integrity and great FAITH!

Every woman that God created must understand that "when all else fails, FAITH will get you there."

~ Peggie Mae Hall

To the Reader

As you read this spirit-filled book of poetry, allow the love of God to penetrate your heart and captivate your spirit. God is waiting on you to activate your FAITH. I say to you, "Be full of FAITH" because when life is at its worst… God is at His best. God is moved by our FAITH. It's time to move forward, and when all else fails, FAITH will get your there.

About the Cover

The book cover is designed to represent how FAITH can be passed on from generation to generation. The eight butterflies are symbolic of how the FAITH in my family was passed on from my ancestors to my parents...from my parents to me...and how I will pass it on to future generations. As it is said in the book of Romans 10:17: "Faith comes from hearing the message, and the message is heard through the Word of Christ."

Table of Contents

A New Beginning

The stage has been set;
the blessings are flowing in
And there's a new beginning—
just around the bend.

Every step takes me closer—
to a higher place in You
Each day takes me farther—
from the things I used to do.

Day by day I'm drawing—
closer to the greatness You've placed in me;
Every minute I cry out:
"Lord let me walk closer to Thee."

Every second I remember—
just how good you are.
My blessings once seemed a long way off—
But now they're not that far.

The stage has been set;
the blessings are flowing in
So many blessings wait on me—
just around the bend.

Lord you promised me health—
showed me how to live a life free from sin;
Lord you have given me victory—
you've placed a Mountain Mover within.

Each hour I'm a little bit—
closer to my expected end;
There are so many blessings waiting—
just around the bend.

I can have anything
that your words proclaim;
You told me I could have what I want—
If I ask it in Jesus' Name.

Wealth is mine, joy is mine,
and peace belongs to me
Can't depend on my physical eyes—
I look with *faith* to Thee.

And Lord you said you'd fight my battle—
on you I can depend;
There are so many blessings—
waiting just around the bend.

My healing "Around the Bend"
My Hope "Around the Bend"
My Joy "Around the Bend"
My Deliverance "Around the Bend"
My Peace "Around the Bend"

A Tear or Two

I can shed a Tear or Two
When I think of all the things that life can do.
But a smile comes on my face
When I think of God's Amazing Grace.

A tear for mom I had to cry
It broke my heart to say good-bye;
But in my pain I found some pleasure
And joy beyond any measure.

For mom's pain—she could not bear;
She was indeed in deep despair
Now for my mom I can smile
Although it took a little while.

Yes, I can shed a tear or two
About all the things that life can do.
But a smile comes upon my face
When I think of God's Amazing Grace.

The day my dad received his burns
The severity was of great concern.
His pain—it grieved my heart so bad
And yes, it made me very sad.

But through faith, my dad is well;
A miracle within him dwells.
Because of him I, too, am blessed;
That makes me smile, I must confess.

Yes, I can shed a tear or two
About all the things that life can do.
But a smile comes upon my face
When I think of God's Amazing Grace.

A baby put aside to die
The infant's mom—she had to cry.
Born three months early, you see;
That infant child was really me.

No incubator to place me in
Very few Negroes could use them then.
But Grandma didn't pay the ol' doctor no mind
She believed that I would be—just fine.

Yes, I can shed a tear or two
About all the things that life can do.
But a smile comes upon my face
When I think of God's Amazing Grace.

When my daughter was very small
She developed pneumonia as I recall.
Off to the hospital we went
Only to be---to another one sent.

Hospital number two said that she was fine,
Yet I knew in my heart that they were lying.
As we were about to go,
An angel appeared—don't you know...

And said, "This child is as sick as can be"
So we carried her on to hospital number three.
There God's Amazing Grace stepped in—
And made me smile once again.

Yes, I can shed a tear or two
About all the things that life can do.
But a smile comes upon my face
When I think of God's Amazing Grace.

A few years ago, I could have gone berserk;
My husband cut his hand in half at work.
The doctor feared he'd lose his hand
But God's Grace was in the Plan.

Now his hand is doing well;
That makes me smile; ☺ Can't you tell?
I thank the Lord for His Healing Power
And for FAITH to stand in the roughest hour.

Yes, I can shed a tear or two
About all the things that life can do.
But a smile comes upon my face
When I think of God's Amazing Grace.

My oldest daughter broke her arm
In several pieces—that caused great alarm
The doctor thought her arm was doomed
For he was thinking about despair and gloom.

But I put a smile upon my face
As I thought of God's Amazing Grace.
It was a chance for my FAITH to grow
Her arm is now stronger than before.

Yes, I can shed a tear or two
About all the things that life can do.
I remember God's Amazing Grace
And put a smile upon my face.
I put a smile upon my face.

A Word or Two

Pray…
Pray Always.

Trust…
Trust Totally.

Live…
Live Abundantly.

Believe…
Believe Intentionally.

Ask…
Ask Boldly.

Meditate…
Meditate Daily.

Know…
Know God.

FAITH…
FAITH forever.

Already Gift-Wrapped

Let Satan Jaw Jack all he wants to;
Let his lips flap.
Honey, every blessing I have for you
Is already gift-wrapped.

Let him deceive all he wants to,
but don't you give in;
Cause I'm gonna keep on blessing you,
time and time again.

Let him lie all he wants;
That's the only thing he does well.
You just wait on your blessings,
Because your God will never fail.

I own the cattle of a thousand hills,
Got gold mines that have never been tapped.
Honey, I've got your blessings waiting on you,
They're already gift-wrapped.

So don't let go of your hopes,
'cuz he can't steal what you've got;
I'm the ruler of this universe,
but he thinks he knows what's hot!

Everything here is mine…
The land, the sea, the sky.
I've got blessings waiting on you;
That there ain't enough money to buy.

So let Satan keep his mouth running;
He does that all the time;
But there's one thing I want to make clear—
He cannot touch what's Mine.

That boy don't want to mess with Me
He knows that he'll get zapped,
Because every blessing I have for you
Is already gift-wrapped.

Good health is yours—prosperity, too.
I even gave you my Son.
Anything else you want—
Just ask, and it shall be done.

Satan only lies and deceives;
He wants you to feel trapped;
But I've got blessings waiting on you…
And they're already gift-wrapped.

Bind/Loose

Bind	Loose
Arrogance	Anointing
Bickering	Balance
Complaining	Commitment to Christ
Depression	Deliverance
Esteem (Low-self)	Excellence
Fear	Favor
Guilt	Grace
Hopelessness	Healing/Hope
Ignorance	Integrity/Intelligence
Jealousy	Joy
Kill joy	Kindness
Lust/Lies	Love/Liberty
Mediocrity	Miracles/Meditation
Nothingness	Newness of Life
Obscenity/Oppression	Obedience/Organization
Pessimism	Power/Prosperity
Quick-Temper	Quality Praise
Resentment/Revenge	Righteousness/Revelation
Stress	Strength
Temptation	Truth
Unbelief/Uncertainty	Unity
Victim Mentality	Virtuousness/Vigor
Weakness/Worry	Wisdom
EXcuses	EXercise
Yourself	Your Purpose
Zaniness/Zelch	Zest/Zeal

Carry the Torch

The torch is passed on to you, my son;
Use it how you see fit.
All those precious times we spent together—
you shall not forget.

I know you'll show my honor well—
in all you say and do;
And you will surely carry on,
and help our family through.

I was blessed during my stay—
they were truly wonderful years,
So clear your eyes—I'm fine—
and wipe away your tears.

Take care of your family—
keep them close to you, my son;
God will reward you, too,
when all your work is done.

You were there for me,
so don't you fret or be sad,
Because the love you shared with me
Was one of the greatest gifts I had.

The memories will live forever—
hold them dear—don't let them past;
For I have journeyed home—
to be with Jesus at last.

I love you, son...I always will;
You made me proud, you see.
Someday God will call you home—
then together again we'll be.

Carry this torch I'm passing to you;
I know you'll do the best that you can;
And someday we will surely see
one another again.

Cutting Down Those Mountains

Cut down those mountains
They're not as high as they seem;
Cut down those mountains
And fulfill your dreams.

Cut down those mountains
Learn to deal with strife;
Cut down those mountains
And get on with your life.

Cut down those mountains
Learn to do your very best;
Cut down those mountains
And you will stand the test.

Cut down those mountains
You have the power within;
Cut down those mountains
Time and time again

Cut down those mountains
They are really not that high
Cut down those mountains
Cut them down…and now FLY!

Every Drop Was Shed For Me

Though sometimes I'm in deep despair
and burdens weigh me down…

Sometimes I get so discouraged…
I feel level to the ground.

Sometimes I'm bound by my illness…
and pain won't set me free.

I'm reminded of the Cross, where Jesus…
shed His blood for me.

He was the only one…
no one else could pay the price.

He shed His precious blood for me…
He was a Holy Sacrifice.

I will keep looking to Jesus…
in Him I have the Victory.

Because every drop of blood He shed,
Every drop was shed for me.
Every drop was shed for me.

Every Woman a Multitude

M = Mother (Life Bearer)
U = Unit/Unity – (Bring things together)
L = Love Lesson (Unconditional love)
T = Teacher (Manners/practice)
I = Intercessor (Prays for others)
T = Truth Teller (Set free)
U = Umbrella (Opens/Covers/Shields)
D = Daughter (Cycle of Blessings)
E = Encourage (You can do it)

In every woman,
a multitude is found.
It doesn't matter how you look
or how you sound;

You're a symbol of peace,
A container of love...
Sent from the Father,
in Heaven above.

You are a multitude!
For you were blessed at your arrival—
God's special creation—
Designed for survival.

You are a multitude
Of Love, Joy, Hope, and FAITH.

Fast-Forward FAITH

Fast-forward your FAITH
When you face challenges, no matter what kind
Keep on 'keeping on'
FAITH can ease your troubled mind.

Hang on to that steadfast FAITH
From God you will receive a reward
Use the Word for life's battles
For the Holy Bible is your sword.

FAITH is the substance of things hoped for
The evidence of things out of sight
Just call on the name of Jesus
And demons will be put to flight.

Fast-Forward
F
A
I
T
H

FAITH moves mountains,
disease and so much more.
Just ask in FAITH and it shall be given
FAITH is the key to unlock the door.

FAITH has parted the seas, shut the mouth of lions
And even made it rain.
FAITH has held back the sun, fed five thousand,
And removed heartaches and pain.

FAITH caused the ravens to feed Elijah
And for Abraham put a ram in the bush
Though Paul sometimes wanted to throw the towel in,
The rewind button he ceased to push.

FAITH can be your bread and water,
Your shelter in a stormy blast...
When all else fails around you...
Be sure your FAITH continues to last!

No matter what you face in life,
No matter how hard it may be,
FAITH will get you through it
It has always worked for me.

Fenced In

Loose me…let me go;
Where I'm going, I do not know.

Unlock the shackles
Remove these chains

My momentum…
I have to regain

Remove these weights
I cannot breathe

Release the limits
I was born to achieve

Barriers you have to break
I don't care about—my past mistakes

Catapult me to my rightful place…
Right in the center Of God's Amazing Grace!

Generations of 'FAITH'

Grandmother was a generation of FAITH...
long suffering and pain--of enduring hard times...
a generation of helping hands,
consideration and patience.

Grandmother was a generation of
boldness, strength, and preciseness.
The love for her children and grandchildren
Surpassed the elements of time.
Her FAITH & determination
was mother's greatest inheritance.

Mother was a generation of hope and inspiration...
a generation which demonstrated the
true meaning of womanhood...
a generation of observation and rectification...
a generation to be recognized and be reckoned with.
Her sense of survival & steadfast FAITH
was my greatest asset.

My generation is a generation of necessity...
A necessity to have great FAITH.

By FAITH, I know that
my child will have a future in this society.

By FAITH, I know that
the survival of black men is a reality.

By FAITH, I know that
the drug situation will get better.

By FAITH, I know that
my generation can rectify the wrong we have done
in parenting our children.

By FAITH, I know that
my hope for better generations
in the years to come will not die.

My daughters' generation will be
a generation of even greater FAITH,
because Great Grandmother had FAITH, Grandmother had FAITH,
and I will pass on my FAITH
to the next generation.

God Does Not Lie

When you told me of your illness
I didn't know what to say.

Then the quiet, sweet voice of Jesus whispered,
"Take some time to kneel and pray."

So I did just what He told me.
My prayer was answered that same night.

Jesus whispered once more and told me:
"Your sister will be alright."

The peace of God came upon me.
My troubled mind was put at ease.

Because I knew the Master Doctor—
Could cure all sickness and disease.

Sweet 'sister', don't you worry.
Sweet 'sister', don't you cry.
God will do just what he promised
And I'm so glad that GOD DOES NOT LIE.

God is Determined to Bless Me

Satan, you don't have any—
Control over my life.
I can speak the Word of God—
Over temptation, trials and strife.

Satan, you are a liar,
Yes, lying is what you do.
I'm not the least bit worried—
Because my God will carry me through.

I don't need your approval;
I operate on FAITH, you see.
I know without a doubt,
that God is determined to bless me.

You may try to bring me down;
Do just what you will.
But I can shout to the mountaintop;
"Peace, be still."

Go ahead and talk about me;
Frankly, I don't care.
I can go to God;
All of my burdens, He'll help me bear.

You can try to put me in chains;
God's Word will set me free.
I know, without a doubt;
God is determined to bless me.

God Speaks

Through a Baby's Cry
A lullaby
Summer's Rain
Aches and Pain
Mountain Peaks
God Speaks.

Through Lightening Strikes
Starlit Nights
Humming Birds
Voices Unheard
God Speaks.

Through a Lonely Day
Heads of Gray
Crowded Homes
Daddy's Gone
God Speaks.

Through a Heart's Desire
Those Who Inspire
Loud and Clear
Can You Hear?

God Speaks!

Her FAITH Filled the Room

The doctor said it was hopeless;
they stood and shook their head;
But the woman cried out in FAITH
from her lonely hospital bed.

The voice was strong and convincing—
her eyes, painted with tears;
But boldly she lifted her head and said:
"I have no worries or fears.

God will use me for His glory,
of His goodness I'll testify.
I will live and I will be healed—
don't look for me to die.

I have talked with my Creator
And this trial is not for me.
I'll be a testimony of—
how God can set you free!

This affliction came and struck me quickly—
It seemed faster than a blink.
I had no time to doubt or waiver—
barely any time to think.

God's Grace is sufficient—
and has always worked for my good.
I will hold on to His Hand—
as He promised me I could.

I want you to believe and agree—
That my healing is on the way.
I'll stand still and allow God to complete the work
He started in me today.

Please don't grumble or be sad;
or deal with despair or gloom.
I am trusting in my God, you see...
My *FAITH has filled the room*!

I have seen what God can do—
have experienced Him for myself.
He'll be the one I can depend on—
when nothing else is left.

I'm trusting in my Lord,
and by His stripes I'm healed.
Soon I'll rise up from this bed
and do my Master's Will.

Please don't worry 'bout me—
don't entertain despair and gloom,
For I am truly depending on God—
My *FAITH has filled this room*!

I have entered His gates with thanksgiving...
And into His courts with praise.
He promised me that Grace and Mercy
will follow me, all of my days.

I can walk in the company of enemies—
a table He'll prepare.
He sees my pain and hears my cries...
and all my burdens he'll help me bear.

He walked me through the valley...
The shadow of death was at my feet.
I can hear the celestial choir...
see my reflection on the golden street.

I hear the angels singing..."Holy, Holy, Holy..."
through the day and through the night.
But God's voice is saying:
"My Child, hold on...Don't give up without a fight."

There's still too much for you to do
To advance to my kingdom, dear.
I've been moved by your FAITH;
It has overshadowed your fears.

Tell your friends and family not to worry...
Please don't entertain despair or gloom
For I have heard your cries and prayers,
Yes, your *FAITH has filled the room.*

Tell everyone you'll be fine—
that you understand your role;
For you are clearly being used—
to save another soul.

Men and women will be drawn...
to God, when you testify.
You can boast of God's Great Goodness;
On Him you can rely.

His promises are many;
Grab hold of them today.
He is surely able,
to make clear for us, a way.

God wants me to be healthy,
so I asked Him to set me free...
God's goodness is wider than the ocean...
With mercy expanding further than the sea.

God Wants me to know His love;
I asked him to help me understand.
He wants me to walk in FAITH...
so I'll move at His command.

He knows my body...
wrote the manual for my design;
No one else is just like me—
I am one of a kind.

My healing is specific—
can be done by the Master's touch;
He's not like a dose of meds—
where I may get too little or too much.

God doesn't have to wait—
every four hours to relieve my pain;
He knows my allergic tendencies—
and how much oxygen to send to my brain.

He knows how to keep my heart pumping—
Whether I'm asleep or am awake;
He knows when I've had enough—
knows just how much I can take.

Please don't worry about me—
don't entertain despair and gloom;
God has been moved by FAITH...
And His Presence has filled my room.

I am grateful such a mighty God Would be...
Moved by the FAITH of 'little ol' me'.

He's not impressed
with my money, fortune, or fame...
He's moved as I acknowledge
all power in His Name. Amen."

Hide it in Your Heart

When things get tough as they often do
Look to the Word—it will carry you through.
When you think the battle—you cannot win
Look to God's Promises and then cash in.

Remember that all of your needs are met;
If God said it, He will not forget.
Don't worry about any weapon formed against you;
If the enemy digs a ditch he'd better dig two.

God loves us; His Word will not depart;
"Especially when you hide it—
deep down in your heart."

If you want to know God now and then,
just be still;
If you love Him, things will work together for good—yes they will.

When you are feeling down and really need a lift;
Give thanks to God for His unspeakable gifts.
When you are running out of energy
and need a new start;
Grab hold of the Bible
and hide the Word in your heart.

The Word will teach you the way that you should go;
Anything you have need of—God already knows.
All of your fears and doubts God can relieve;
When you absorb His Word...
and have the FAITH to believe.

Hide the Word in your heart
and you will be blessed;
With the heart man believeth;
with the tongue he does confess.

Stay strong in your faith;
and don't you dare doubt;
Let the Word of God—
from your lips proceedeth out.

Let the Word pierce your heart;
hide it anyhow;
Declare the Word
and you're on the right track now.

Hide it deep…
in the secret chambers of your heart;
Every day you can
'Rejoice' for a brand new start.

You are more than a conqueror;
you are a joint heir with Christ;
Just knowing your authority
should make you feel real nice.

Know that only the blood of Jesus
can wash away your sins;
You can count on Jesus—
He truly is your friend.

Take the time to hide the Word in your heart;
do it with all ease;
Remember that from praying…
you should never cease.

The power is within;
I can be whatever I want to be;
I can do all things—
through Christ who strengthens me.

Hide the Word in your heart—
know that every word is true;
You can receive power—
after the Holy Ghost comes on you.

Don't doubt a single word—
no never, never, never;
Let every creature praise—
His Holy Name forever.

The Word will do just
what God said it would do;
He'll give us a new heart—
and put a new spirit within us, too.

Hide the Word in your heart,
the way you do your favorite song;
Let your tongue speak of God's righteousness;
Praise Him all the day long.

Trust God for where you're going;
Thank Him for where you've been;
For He has given you the spirit—
Of power, love, and self-discipline.

Hide the Word in your heart;
the Word's the only choice;
Let your soul be glorified—
and let your spirit rejoice.

Remember Matthew 10:8...
for as long as you live;
It states:
"Freely you have received, freely give."

Hide the Word in your heart—
no matter what folks may say;
Don't lose heart because inwardly,
we're renewed day by day.

Hide the Word in your heart—
every minute of every hour;
Be strong in the Lord,
and in His mighty power.

Remember God's Word—
His Mercy and Goodness will astound.
When the evil day comes—
you'll be able to stand your ground.

Hide the Word in your heart—
your goals you can achieve;
Because everything is possible—
if you only believe.

Hide the Word in your heart;
let it put your mind at ease;
God forgives all of your sins,
and can heal all sickness and disease.

The Word of God gives life—
a new beginning—a brand new start;
If you want to make it through the storms of life—
Hide the Word in your Heart.

I Can't Look Down

When I think about my life
And where I started off;
When I think about my hard times,
I hear a voice—so sweet, so soft.

JESUS is saying,
"My child, hold your head up—I'll always be around."
That's when I realize
I'm too blessed to look down.

When I think about the rough times
That often fill my life,
I think about the heartaches,
the troubles and the strife.

When quitting seems so easy
And there is no joy to be found,
The sweet voice of JESUS whispers:
"Don't you dare look down."

When I lose my loved ones
And sorrow fills my heart,
I must hold firmly to his promises
And from my FAITH I can't depart.

I may smile on the outside—
yet my heart may wear a frown.
I know I've got to keep my head up...
I'm too blessed to look down.

I Love Who You Are

I love who you are; I made you that way.
It's not how you talk—but the things that you say.
I made your thick lips—to worship and praise
To call upon Me—all of your days.
The way that you look—well that's no surprise;
I am the one—who put the slant in your eyes.
Your carmel skin—I hand-picked myself
I decided whether your dominant hand
would be right or left.

The language you speak is unique by design;
I chose you to be—a child of Mine.

The curls in your hair or the straight long flow
That stands still in the wind—or maybe it blows.
The point in your nose—
or how it spreads on your face
Was sculptured by design—
through God's Amazing Grace.

Your mom and your dad—I picked them, too.
Honor and respect them
and long life will be granted to you.

The shape of your hands—the span of your height
Was not a decision that took me all night.
You were sculptured by love—my vessel to fill;
I gave you breath—to do my Holy Will.

If you decide to go another way
Don't be surprised on that great Judgement Day.
For truly I love you—you're one of a kind;
Sculptured with precision—a unique design.

No matter the skin color, creed, or race,
I put you in time, and selected your space.
To live out your dreams—to walk in My Plan
You were created by Me—woman or man.

Faith is a factor;
love is the key;
Jesus is the Light;
The Connection is Me.

I'll Be Ready to Leave

One day I'll give up this earthly body
And head for my heavenly home.

You don't have to shed a single tear
I won't be sad I'm gone.

Don't you fret, my friend, or
hang your head low.

Don't tell my family
You're sad to see me go.

Don't send cards and flowers
To say your last good-bye.

And please don't waste no time at all
To ask the Master, "why?"

I've been blessed with untold riches
From my Heavenly Father above.

I've been showered with His goodness
I've been wrapped up in His love.

I truly mean this with all my heart
And trust you will believe.

That when I leave my earthly home
I'll Be Ready To Leave.

Jesus, I Love You

Jesus, I'm waiting for your return.
I want to hear your voice say,
"Good and faithful servant, well done."

I know you'll do
everything your word proclaims;
That's why I will continue to praise your Holy Name.

I want to be caught up
when the trumpets blow.
I won't have to cry—or be misunderstood anymore.

I'm living this life just to be with You someday.
I said I love you, Jesus…and God's Word I will obey.
I have to give up—the wrong for the right;
Sometimes I may even—have some restless nights.

I'm holding on to you, Jesus;
I know the Word of God is true.
You are everything I need—
Jesus, I Love You!

Mirrors of the Heart

I heard a sad song today.
It made me think of you.
The thing that was the saddest
Is that the song was really true.

It spoke about the heartaches
that sometimes come our way...
about the pain we might encounter
on any given day...

How the trials of life cause suffering,
tribulations and despair...
and that a friend named Jesus
For all our burdens He will bear.

I heard a sad song today.
It made me think of you.
Oh how I wish with all my heart
That sad song wasn't true.

I saw a pretty smile today
A smile so warm and sincere.
The smile would soon start to fade,
yet it looked so clear.

It was the loveliest smile I've ever seen
in all of my years;
But somehow that lovely smile
Was washed away by tears.

I held a lovely rose today...
the petals were bursting with red;
But in my heart I wished...
that rose had been you, instead.

So I held on to that rose...
and reflected on your face;
Because the Mirrors of my Heart
Have reserved for you, a very special place.

Night's Song

Sweetness
Serenity
Safety
Soul

Melancholy
Majestic
Mesmerizing
Mild

Enlightening
Enticing
Evolving
Excursion

Lively
Librating
Love-filled
Lasting

Lingering
Longevity
Lamentable
Listen

To the Night's Song
SMELL the Tranquility

Out of Step

Sometimes the walk gets lonely;
And the way gets a little bit hard.
Sometimes the road gets weary
No one seems to do their part.

Now and then we get a little down and out
'Cuz we don't call 'up' for our help.
It's time to get back in the Word,
Line up—you're 'Out of Step.'

Sometimes we lose loved ones—
And it seems like nothing's left.
Sometimes we have to do like David—
And take time to encourage ourselves.

Sometimes we get knocked down—
Like Saul on the Damascus Road
Sometimes we are like Jonah—
We must get thrown overboard.

Now and then we wallow in self-pity
It's time to call upon our help.
It's time to get back in focus—
Line up with Jesus when you're Out of Step.

Latch on to Jesus, when you're Out of Step
Out of Step
Out of Step
Out of Step
Out of Step
Line up to the Word—look up to the Hills

Lean back and relax...Lean on Jesus—
You're Out of Step.
Line up—line up—line up—
lean on Jesus when you're "Out of Step."

Pick it Up

One Wednesday night I went into my kitchen
To get a bite to eat...
not knowing what I wanted...
just a little treat.

As I opened up the refrigerator
A soft voice I heard,
"You really don't want that food.
You're hungry for the Word."

I pretended not to hear
what the voice had said;
Then I asked myself:
"How long has it been since the Bible you have read?"

I decided to ignore
what the voice had to say;
I turned to my refrigerator
to grab some food anyway.

I closed the refrigerator
and was about to leave that place
What but the Holy Bible
was staring me in the face.

This was no coincidence;
it was really meant to be.
I never keep my Bible in my kitchen...
Can't you see?

I picked up my Bible
to see what I could find.
Would you believe St. Mark, Chapter 13
came to mind?

I began reading;
each word meant so much.
Before I could turn the page…
my heart was deeply touched.

So whenever you get an urge to eat,
or to drink from a cup,
reach for some spiritual food in your Bible—
It's waiting there—just *Pick It Up*.

She Traveled It

She traveled the road of life;
she gave her best each day.
She walked the walk and talked the talk,
to help others find their way.

She traveled the road of life
with its many curves and turns.
The occasional potholes she faced,
were opportunities for us to learn.

She was destined to complete her journey;
God charted which path she would take.
She was fully aware of the difference
she was placed on this earth, to make!

She just kept on traveling through the storm,
and also through the rain.
And many times as she traveled,
she saw hurt disappointment, and pain.

She stayed focused, she pressed hard,
dug deeper, and took a stand.
She moved as the Spirit led,
adjusting her speed at God's command.

Our traveling friend was persistent,
she was determined to finish the course.
Embracing us, Trusting God, Abiding In His word;
In God she had found her source.

She traveled the road of life with laughter,
and around the room she would dance.
She traveled with love and open arms,
and gave others a second chance.

She traveled the road of teaching,
picked up passengers who could not read.
She never gave up or pushed others away;
she believed we all could succeed.

She would often travel light;
Humanity was her crew.
She helped us travel through many situations;
we needed to press our way through.

She traveled the road of life,
purpose and passion she used as fuel.
She traveled the road of commitment,
and honesty and love were her tools.

The road our friend was traveling
took a sudden twist.
We know God is in control,
yet our friend we will deeply miss.

She left us an example
of her travel plan in detail.
Her directions simply state,
"When you are traveling With God you cannot fail."

Something Big

I want to do something big
I'm tired of sitting on my butt

I want to do something big
But I really don't know what

Big things are really exciting
But I'm not fascinated by their size

There's just one very small thing
That we all must realize

Big things are done
In tiny little steps

Writing down your goal
Truly does help

If you do the little things
With determination and persistence

The big thing will appear
With a lot less resistance

Remember it's okay
To want to do things in a grand style

But be sure to hold onto the little things
They'll add up after a while.

Standing In My Dream

It can't be real; it can't be true
Accomplishing everything you set out to do

It can't be happening; this is not real
I can't believe how good this feels

It's so awesome, I want to scream
I'm standing right here—in my dream.

I did not know which day it would be
When my vision could catch up with me.

I saw myself here every day
I practiced every word I'd say.

Lovelier than a crystal stream
I'm standing right here—in my dream.

I know for certain that God Is the key;
He showed me all that I could not see.

He placed this passion deep within
And gave me favor with Him and men.

With Him, I had the perfect team;
I'm standing right here—in my dream.

Sunday Morning On Our Minds

We have had some smooth sailing.
We have also had bumpy spots.
We have crossed over a few bridges.
We have not always had a lot.

We have been faced with a few disasters.
Discontentment has had its turn.
We have had some hard days
But they will never outweigh the good ones.

We held our heads up and kept moving.
We continued to tow the line.
We had to keep our hearts in motion,
Because Sunday Morning was on our minds.

We have continued on the path we are traveling.
The road goes up and sometimes down.
We have encountered many faces...
Some with smiles and some with frowns.

It does not matter what we've had to encounter.
We knew that we would be just fine...
Because there is one thing for certain,
Sunday Morning was on our minds.

We passed by doubt and discouragement;
Heartache and pain played their parts.
But we just had to keep on going
Because serving God was in our hearts.

So we robed ourselves with hope
And put the shield of faith in our hands.
Although we moved by different measures,
We all moved at God's command.

It matters not what the problem
We're gonna let our little lights shine.
We're gonna keep on trusting in Jesus
Because Sunday Morning is on our minds.

Sunday morning keeps us encouraged
Monday through Saturday night.
Because we know the Holy Spirit
Will help us treat each other right.

We will deal with our weekly dilemmas;
Satan will surely bind...
Because there's one thing for certain...
We've got Sunday Morning on our minds!

We've got Sunday Morning On Our Minds!

Talk to Me, Lord

Advice needed...
Message
not heard...

Sound is foggy...
Respond
in a word...

Letters unanswered...
Calls
not returned...

Whisper softly...
Many
concerns...

Answer quickly...
I'm waiting
on you...

Talk to me, Lord...
What
shall I do?

Thank God I Don't Look Like What I've Been Through

It looks like things are together—
Like I don't have a trouble in the world.
I look like all is well
And I'm a happy and vibrant girl.

I look like I've got it 'going on'
And my life is glamour and glory.
What I look like and what I've been through
Is a totally different story.

I've been through the loss of a mother,
From dad, the doc walked away and shook his head;
But through it all, God would make a way;
He knows our thoughts—what we do and say.

God will help us make it through
On Him we can depend
He set us free from guilt and shame
That we know results from sin.

He's a great and merciful Father
Wraps us in His beautiful grace;
Sets our spirit free to praise
And sets a smile upon our face.

We would look like hopeless children
If God did not intervene
Because life can really wear you down
And people can be so mean.

I don't look like what I've been through,
And to me that is no surprise;
God is our source of strength…
And THAT we need to recognize.

The Flip Side of Commitment

UNCOMMITTED

Strange • Defenseless • Overshadowing • Pain

Misery • Pressure • Powerless • Disdain

Confusion • Chaos • Insanity • Grief

Superficial • Sensation • Imprisoned • No Relief

COMMITTED

Pleasure • Love • Hope • Success

Exciting • Joyful • Happiness • Blessed

Dreams • Fulfilled • Doing It • Together

Through Sunshine • Soft Rains

Gliding Through Inclimate Weather

When we commit our lives to God…
He commits His abundant blessings to us.

Traffic Signals of Life

Stop your lying and your fussing
And your gossiping on the phone.
Say "Get thee behind me, Satan—
just leave me alone!"

Stop standing by
when your brother needs a helping hand.
Reach out in the name of Jesus—
And help your fellow man.

Stop holding a grudge
For ten and twenty years.
Learn to say, "I'm sorry,"
And wipe away your tears.

Stop waiting for others to do their part;
Do what you can—with a free and willing heart.

Stop being lost, but declare, "I'm found!"
Refuse to stand on shaky ground.

Stop living for Satan—whatever you do!
Slow down on the way—and tell a friend or two.

Slow down and tell them—what God can do;
You certainly ought to know—He's been good to you.

Slow down and tell them—
that Jesus is all they need;
Just ask in Jesus' name…
their hungry souls He'll feed.

Slow down and tell them
that Jesus is the lawyer that never lost a case;
He'll help you fight your battle—
and help you run this race.

Tell them they don't have to worry
about inflation or how far a dollar can go;
That Jesus will make a way (out of no way)
Because He loves us so.

Slow down and tell them
That the time is now.
Just trust in Jesus—
His Word will show you how.

Tell them they don't have to worry—
they don't have to fret;
That my God has never
failed me yet.

Slow down for a minute—
and lend a helping hand;
and get ready to go with me—
to the Promised Land.

Go tell the world
about the God you serve;
Tell them He'll give them—
the second chance that they deserve.

Go tell them that He died—and He rose again;
How He set us free—from the death of sin.

Go tell them how He healed the lame
and gave sight to the blind;
Tell them He's the best friend—
any man can find.

(Speak of the miracles)
about the two little fish and five loaves of bread—
how Jesus blessed the food—
and a multitude was fed.

Tell them of His love—
so perfect and so true.
How He said, "Do unto others—
as you would have them do unto you."

Go tell them of the joy that Jesus gives;
That He's not dead, but the Savior lives.

That Jesus is a friend…when your friends are gone;
How He'll make your enemies leave you alone.

Go tell them about His peace and unmerited grace;
That you long to see Him face to face.

Tell them He'll stick by you…
when the going gets rough;
How He'll take care of your enemies—
when they get tough.

Go out and tell them and mean it from your heart;
That none but the righteous shall see God.

Tell them that Jesus loves them…
That he really, really cares;
All of our burdens,
He will help us bear.

Go say to the world,
"I'll pay the price
that my green light is on…
I'll live for Christ!"

It matters not—
what the traffic signals of life may be;
I live for Christ…
and Christ lives in me.

Turn the Pages and Live

Life is a process
Every day you can be blessed
It depends upon what you confess
So put your mouth to the test.

Life is an avenue
There are things you have to go through
How you handle it is up to you
Now what are you going to do?

Life is a precious gift
When others you help to lift
From His Word you never drift
From a life of sin you continue to shift.

Life is eternal
If you believe Christ died for your sin
He rose again, to save all men.
So let your Christian walk begin.

Life is splendor
His grace and mercy are so tender
Faithful service you must render
And your life you must surrender

Take a chance on life!
Turn the Pages and Live!

Two Minute Warning

In need of a blessing
So I'll fall on my knees
And cry out to the Lord
Won't you have mercy on me, please!

I'm in need of a miracle
And my soul is yearning
I have heard the two-minute warning.

I can't make it physically
To the place I need to be
Holy Spirit,
will you show up for me?

Lord, if it's your will
I know it shall be done
So I'll step back and watch
You show out on this one.

I'll be still for sure,
Because you're in control
You're truly the captain of my soul.

Lord, you know exactly what's best for me
My life will become what you intend it to be.

I'll 'be still' Lord, while you take the lead
For your Plan says that "I will succeed."

Those things that may seem Impossible for me
Are nothing but a simple act for 'Thee'.

The alarm has sounded
and the clock keeps ticking
Failure—man is predicting.

But God, there's not failure—
no, not in You.
Please do it Lord...
I know you'll 'See it Through.'

I'm waiting , Lord, with great expectation;
I know we are in right relation;
I'm trusting You, my FAITH has kicked in;
You've done it before, Lord, Do it Again!

Unleash the "Finisher" in You

This is the year of the "Finisher"...
don't start what you don't plan to do.
This is the year to release completion...
the year to follow through.

All those things you've dreamed of...
don't "wish you could" another day.
All you have to do is dive right in...
this isn't the year for delay.

Those things you've put aside...
because you thought the task was too great...
Or perhaps you said, "I can't do it...
I've waited just a little too late."

Shake off your fears and dust off your doubts...
your season is finally here.
The fog has finally lifted...
your vision is crystal clear.

This is the year of the "Finisher"...
and through God you will achieve.
You must put your feet to the fire...
You must have FAITH to believe.

Get up, get ready, and get going...
Don't allow your dreams to diminish
Before you begin what you've 'lone to do...
Visualize that task finished.

Don't let your critics persuade you...
that your task cannot be done.
Don't stop your dream for those who might say,
"Wait for a bigger one."

God has placed purpose within you.
He has blessed your hands and your feet.
Know that your result is victory…
God never intended defeat.

Your work is all around you.
Your destiny is closing in.
Your past defeats do not matter…
This is your year to win.

This is the year of the "Finisher."
Are you willing to stay in the race?
If so, turn up your praise and worship…
And start praying at a steady pace.

Latch on to your Purpose…
And clothe yourself with hope.
When major challenges come your way…
Know that with God, you can cope.

He's put victory inside of you…
He's selected your desires with care.
And whenever you face a mountain…
Release the mountain mover—He's in there!

God has equipped you with staying power…
He's placed "The Finisher" within.
Rely on the Word and the Holy Spirit
to help you complete every task that you begin.

Victory Smells So Sweet

I've stood in the midst of the giants
Rubbed elbows with the best
Life has been full of challenges
I was prepared to stand my test.

I've walked the halls with royalty
Dined with the cream of the crop
I've been stroked with encouragement
And My FAITH won't let me stop.

I've sat at a table with knowledge
I took patience for my friend
Wisdom made me realize
That we're playing this game to win.

I've been met with hatred
But made kindness my choice
I've learned it's not what you say
It's the way you use your voice.

I've played this game of life to win
I've never feared defeat
And when the final call is made
Victory Will Smell So Sweet!

Walking Through – Working it Out

Though I walk through the Valley,
The shadow of death is all around.
God is working things out;
He will never let me down.

Though men may slay me with
The lies they choose to tell,
God is working things out—
He will never let me fail.

Though sickness tries to penetrate
My dwelling at a constant pace,
God will grant me health and prosperity
If I continue to seek His face.

Though my friends will forsake me
And come against my dreams,
God will provide a way of escape
No matter how things may seem.

Though the economy appears to fail
And gas prices rise at a steady beat,
God has already rendered me victories—
In Him there's no defeat.

Though pestilences may try to find us,
With our faith a little low,
God has established a standard—
A place of nurture—a place to grow.

Though we may get weary and wonder…
Just what we can't live without,
Never, ever lose your focus—
The Holy Spirit is Walking Through—Working it Out!

What Shall You Give In Exchange For Your FAITH?

What Shall You Give
In Exchange For Your FAITH?
Will you give Love in the form of a
Beautiful Queen, A Sweet Spirit, and a Bold Believer?

What Shall You Give
In Exchange For Your FAITH?
Will you give Hope in the form of a
Melody in spring, a Rainbow after the Storm,
and a Lasting Peace?

What Shall You Give
In Exchange For Your FAITH?
Will you give Grace in a Loving Touch,
A Radiant Smile, and a Strong Stand?

What Shall You Give
In Exchange For Your FAITH?
Will you give Mercy in a Willingness to demonstrate,
A Positive Attitude, and an Honesty beyond belief?

What Shall You Give
In Exchange For Your FAITH?
Will you give Comfort to
Share the Burdens of Others,
And Pray faithfully for Your Brothers and Sisters?

What Shall You Give
In Exchange For Your FAITH?
Will you give Peace in the form of
a Quiet Sweet Voice, an Encouraging Word,
and Holiness to live right?

What Shall You Give
In Exchange For Your FAITH?
Will you give Bountiful Blessings,
an unwavering Compassion,
and a Light that reflects the Love of Christ?

What Shall You Give
In Exchange For Your FAITH?
Will you give the Desires of your Heart,
Water-Walking Convictions,
and Mountain-Moving Strength?

What Shall You Give In Exchange For Your FAITH?

Wings On My Mind

I've got Wings on my Mind
Move out of my way—it's Praising Time
I can't lie around anymore
Got to get up—this very hour
Because a Problem turns to Praise
When I use my Power.

I've got Wings on my Mind
Move out of my way—it's Praying Time
It's time to fall down on my knees—
Cry out, "Lord, help me, please!"
He's sending an answer—this very hour
'Cause a Problem turns to Praise
When I use my Power.

I've got Wings on my Mind
Move out of my way—it's Shouting Time
I can't sit here and be still anymore
I've gotta dance for Jesus
He has blessed me so
God is making a way—this very hour
'Cause a Problem turns to Praise
When I use my Power.

I've got Wings on my Mind
Move out of my way—it's Trusting Time
I've gotta believe what He promised in His Word
The things I've seen—things I've heard.
God will do what His Word says He will do;
Move out of my way—and I will not block you.
He's turning things around—at this very hour
'Cause a Problem turns to Praise
When I use my Power.

Would It Be Better

Would it be better not to teach than to know the
gut-wrenching pain
Of not being effective with students?

Would it be better not to talk than to spread the
hatred and evil thoughts
You have about your brothers and sisters?

Would it be better not to see
than to witness the destruction, tolerance,
complacency and willingness to do nothing?

Would it be better not to feel
Than to feel the lowliness of heart, grief,
pain and suffering
Of those you have grown to love?

Would it be better not to hope
Than to wish others fail, live in hopelessness,
Or have no vision or dream?

Would it be better not to hear
Than to be inundated with negativity,
Doused with seeds of bitterness
Or daunted with words like,
"they can't" or "they won't?"

Would it be better not to love
Than to withstand the soberness of injustice, cruelty,
And evil lurking about?

We see, but don't see;
We hear, but don't hear;
We feel, but don't feel;
We love, but don't love;
We have hope, yet appear hopeless.
We teach, but never really learn.

Have we bowed down to the belief that all is lost?...
Escaped to an island of numbness,
or defected from the
Human phenomenon of change?

Oh ye of little FAITH.

You Can't Move Forward Because You Keep Looking Back

Let go of your sorrow
Let go of your shame.

Hold your head up high
And strut on in Jesus' name.

You must be encouraged
You keep holding on,

And before you know it
All of your sadness will be gone.

Let go of the darkness
Hold fast to your dreams,

And when you really need to holler
Just release a loud scream.

Walk faster and faster
And the past will fade away.

Look forward to tomorrow
It will be a better day.

FAITH is an action you're empowered to share;
When all else fails…FAITH will get you there.

Preface to Fast-Forward FAITH Journal

"Have faith in God," Jesus answered.
"I tell you the truth, if anyone says to this
mountain, 'Go, throw yourself into the sea,'
and does not doubt in his heart
but believes that what he says will happen,
it will be done for him."
Mark 11: 22-23

"Believe me when I say that I am in the Father
and the Father is in me;
or at least believe on the evidence
of the miracles themselves.
I tell you the truth, anyone who has faith in Me
will do what I have been doing.
He will do even greater things than these,
because I am going to the Father.
And I will do whatever you ask in my name,
so that the Son may bring glory to the Father."
John 14: 11-13

Fast-Forward FAITH Journal

Daily Reflection

FAITH-FILLED Rooms

How has your FAITH changed the atmosphere in the places you have dwelled today?

Fast-Forward
FAITH Journal

Daily Reflection

FAITH-FILLED Rooms

How has your FAITH changed the atmosphere in the places you have dwelled today?

Fast-Forward FAITH Journal

Daily Reflection

FAITH-FILLED Rooms

How has your FAITH changed the atmosphere in the places you have dwelled today?

Fast-Forward FAITH Journal

Daily Reflection

FAITH-FILLED Rooms

How has your FAITH changed the atmosphere in the places you have dwelled today?

Fast-Forward
FAITH Journal

Daily Reflection

FAITH-FILLED Rooms

How has your FAITH changed the atmosphere in the places you have dwelled today?

Fast-Forward
FAITH Journal

Daily Reflection

FAITH-FILLED Rooms

How has your FAITH changed the atmosphere in the places you have dwelled today?

Fast-Forward FAITH Journal

Daily Reflection

FAITH-FILLED Rooms

How has your FAITH changed the atmosphere in the places you have dwelled today?

Fast-Forward
FAITH Journal

Weekly Reflection

What FAITH-FILLED testimonies have been passed on in your home this week?

...in your workplace?

...in your place of worship?

Fast-Forward
FAITH Journal

Daily Reflection

FAITH-FILLED Rooms

How has your FAITH changed the atmosphere in the places you have dwelled today?

Fast-Forward
FAITH Journal

Daily Reflection

FAITH-FILLED Rooms

How has your FAITH changed the atmosphere in the places you have dwelled today?

Fast-Forward
FAITH Journal

Daily Reflection

FAITH-FILLED Rooms

How has your FAITH changed the atmosphere in the places you have dwelled today?

Fast-Forward FAITH Journal

Daily Reflection

FAITH-FILLED Rooms

How has your FAITH changed the atmosphere in the places you have dwelled today?

Fast-Forward FAITH Journal

Daily Reflection

FAITH-FILLED Rooms

How has your FAITH changed the atmosphere in the places you have dwelled today?

Fast-Forward FAITH Journal

Daily Reflection

FAITH-FILLED Rooms

How has your FAITH changed the atmosphere in the places you have dwelled today?

Fast-Forward
FAITH Journal

Daily Reflection

FAITH-FILLED Rooms

How has your FAITH changed the atmosphere in the places you have dwelled today?

Fast-Forward FAITH Journal

Weekly Reflection

What FAITH-FILLED testimonies have been passed on in your home this week?

...in your workplace?

...in your place of worship?

Fast-Forward FAITH Journal

Daily Reflection

FAITH-FILLED Rooms

How has your FAITH changed the atmosphere in the places you have dwelled today?

Fast-Forward
FAITH Journal

Daily Reflection

FAITH-FILLED Rooms

How has your FAITH changed the atmosphere in the places you have dwelled today?

Fast-Forward
FAITH Journal

Daily Reflection

FAITH-FILLED Rooms

How has your FAITH changed the atmosphere in the places you have dwelled today?

Fast-Forward FAITH Journal

Daily Reflection

FAITH-FILLED Rooms

How has your FAITH changed the atmosphere in the places you have dwelled today?

Fast-Forward
FAITH Journal

Daily Reflection

FAITH-FILLED Rooms

How has your FAITH changed the atmosphere in the places you have dwelled today?

Fast-Forward
FAITH Journal

Daily Reflection

FAITH-FILLED Rooms

How has your FAITH changed the atmosphere in the places you have dwelled today?

Fast-Forward
FAITH Journal

Daily Reflection

FAITH-FILLED Rooms

How has your FAITH changed the atmosphere in the places you have dwelled today?

Fast-Forward
FAITH Journal

Weekly Reflection

What FAITH-FILLED testimonies have been passed on in your home this week?

...in your workplace?

...in your place of worship?

Fast-Forward
FAITH Journal

Daily Reflection

FAITH-FILLED Rooms

How has your FAITH changed the atmosphere in the places you have dwelled today?

Fast-Forward
FAITH Journal

Daily Reflection

FAITH-FILLED Rooms

How has your FAITH changed the atmosphere in the places you have dwelled today?

Fast-Forward
FAITH Journal

Daily Reflection

FAITH-FILLED Rooms

How has your FAITH changed the atmosphere in the places you have dwelled today?

Fast-Forward
FAITH Journal

Daily Reflection

FAITH-FILLED Rooms

How has your FAITH changed the atmosphere in the places you have dwelled today?

Fast-Forward
FAITH Journal

Daily Reflection

FAITH-FILLED Rooms

How has your FAITH changed the atmosphere in the places you have dwelled today?

Fast-Forward FAITH Journal

Daily Reflection

FAITH-FILLED Rooms

How has your FAITH changed the atmosphere in the places you have dwelled today?

Fast-Forward FAITH Journal

Daily Reflection

FAITH-FILLED Rooms

How has your FAITH changed the atmosphere in the places you have dwelled today?

Fast-Forward FAITH Journal

Weekly Reflection

What FAITH-FILLED testimonies have been passed on in your home this week?

...in your workplace?

...in your place of worship?

Fast-Forward
FAITH Journal

Daily Reflection

FAITH-FILLED Rooms

How has your FAITH changed the atmosphere in the places you have dwelled today?

Fast-Forward
FAITH Journal

Daily Reflection

FAITH-FILLED Rooms

How has your FAITH changed the atmosphere in the places you have dwelled today?

Fast-Forward
FAITH Journal

Daily Reflection

FAITH-FILLED Rooms

How has your FAITH changed the atmosphere in the places you have dwelled today?

Fast-Forward FAITH Journal

Daily Reflection

FAITH-FILLED Rooms

How has your FAITH changed the atmosphere in the places you have dwelled today?

Fast-Forward
FAITH Journal

Daily Reflection

FAITH-FILLED Rooms

How has your FAITH changed the atmosphere in the places you have dwelled today?

Fast-Forward FAITH Journal

Daily Reflection

FAITH-FILLED Rooms

How has your FAITH changed the atmosphere in the places you have dwelled today?

Fast-Forward FAITH Journal

Daily Reflection

FAITH-FILLED Rooms

How has your FAITH changed the atmosphere in the places you have dwelled today?

Fast-Forward
FAITH Journal

Weekly Reflection

What FAITH-FILLED testimonies have been passed on in your home this week?

...in your workplace?

...in your place of worship?

Fast-Forward
FAITH Journal

Daily Reflection

FAITH-FILLED Rooms

How has your FAITH changed the atmosphere in the places you have dwelled today?

Fast-Forward
FAITH Journal

Daily Reflection

FAITH-FILLED Rooms

How has your FAITH changed the atmosphere in the places you have dwelled today?

Fast-Forward FAITH Journal

Daily Reflection

FAITH-FILLED Rooms

How has your FAITH changed the atmosphere in the places you have dwelled today?

Fast-Forward
FAITH Journal

Daily Reflection

FAITH-FILLED Rooms

How has your FAITH changed the atmosphere in the places you have dwelled today?

Fast-Forward
FAITH Journal

Daily Reflection

FAITH-FILLED Rooms

How has your FAITH changed the atmosphere in the places you have dwelled today?

Fast-Forward
FAITH Journal

Daily Reflection

FAITH-FILLED Rooms

How has your FAITH changed the atmosphere in the places you have dwelled today?

Fast-Forward FAITH Journal

Daily Reflection

FAITH-FILLED Rooms

How has your FAITH changed the atmosphere in the places you have dwelled today?

Fast-Forward
FAITH Journal

Weekly Reflection

What FAITH-FILLED testimonies have been passed on in your home this week?

...in your workplace?

...in your place of worship?

Fast-Forward
FAITH Journal

Daily Reflection

FAITH-FILLED Rooms

How has your FAITH changed the atmosphere in the places you have dwelled today?

Fast-Forward
FAITH Journal

Daily Reflection

FAITH-FILLED Rooms

How has your FAITH changed the atmosphere in the places you have dwelled today?

Fast-Forward FAITH Journal

Daily Reflection

FAITH-FILLED Rooms

How has your FAITH changed the atmosphere in the places you have dwelled today?

Fast-Forward
FAITH Journal

Daily Reflection

FAITH-FILLED Rooms

How has your FAITH changed the atmosphere in the places you have dwelled today?

Fast-Forward
FAITH Journal

Daily Reflection

FAITH-FILLED Rooms

How has your FAITH changed the atmosphere in the places you have dwelled today?

Fast-Forward
FAITH Journal

Daily Reflection

FAITH-FILLED Rooms

How has your FAITH changed the atmosphere in the places you have dwelled today?

Fast-Forward
FAITH Journal

Daily Reflection

FAITH-FILLED Rooms

How has your FAITH changed the atmosphere in the places you have dwelled today?

Fast-Forward
FAITH Journal

Weekly Reflection

What FAITH-FILLED testimonies have been passed on in your home this week?

...in your workplace?

...in your place of worship?

Fast-Forward FAITH Journal

Daily Reflection

FAITH-FILLED Rooms

How has your FAITH changed the atmosphere in the places you have dwelled today?

Fast-Forward
FAITH Journal

Daily Reflection

FAITH-FILLED Rooms

How has your FAITH changed the atmosphere in the places you have dwelled today?

Fast-Forward
FAITH Journal

Daily Reflection

FAITH-FILLED Rooms

How has your FAITH changed the atmosphere in the places you have dwelled today?

Fast-Forward
FAITH Journal

Daily Reflection

FAITH-FILLED Rooms

How has your FAITH changed the atmosphere in the places you have dwelled today?

Fast-Forward
FAITH Journal

Daily Reflection

FAITH-FILLED Rooms

How has your FAITH changed the atmosphere in the places you have dwelled today?

Fast-Forward
FAITH Journal

Daily Reflection

FAITH-FILLED Rooms

How has your FAITH changed the atmosphere in the places you have dwelled today?

Fast-Forward
FAITH Journal

Daily Reflection

FAITH-FILLED Rooms

How has your FAITH changed the atmosphere in the places you have dwelled today?

Fast-Forward
FAITH Journal

Weekly Reflection

What FAITH-FILLED testimonies have been passed on in your home this week?

...in your workplace?

...in your place of worship?

Fast-Forward
FAITH Journal

Daily Reflection

FAITH-FILLED Rooms

How has your FAITH changed the atmosphere in the places you have dwelled today?

Fast-Forward
FAITH Journal

Daily Reflection

FAITH-FILLED Rooms

How has your FAITH changed the atmosphere in the places you have dwelled today?

Fast-Forward
FAITH Journal

Daily Reflection

FAITH-FILLED Rooms

How has your FAITH changed the atmosphere in the places you have dwelled today?

Fast-Forward
FAITH Journal

Daily Reflection

FAITH-FILLED Rooms

How has your FAITH changed the atmosphere in the places you have dwelled today?

Fast-Forward
FAITH Journal

Daily Reflection

FAITH-FILLED Rooms

How has your FAITH changed the atmosphere in the places you have dwelled today?

Fast-Forward FAITH Journal

Daily Reflection

FAITH-FILLED Rooms

How has your FAITH changed the atmosphere in the places you have dwelled today?

Fast-Forward FAITH Journal

Daily Reflection

FAITH-FILLED Rooms

How has your FAITH changed the atmosphere in the places you have dwelled today?

Fast-Forward
FAITH Journal

Weekly Reflection

What FAITH-FILLED testimonies have been passed on in your home this week?

...in your workplace?

...in your place of worship?

Fast-Forward
FAITH Journal

Daily Reflection

FAITH-FILLED Rooms

How has your FAITH changed the atmosphere in the places you have dwelled today?

Fast-Forward
FAITH Journal

Daily Reflection

FAITH-FILLED Rooms

How has your FAITH changed the atmosphere in the places you have dwelled today?

Fast-Forward FAITH Journal

Daily Reflection

FAITH-FILLED Rooms

How has your FAITH changed the atmosphere in the places you have dwelled today?

Fast-Forward FAITH Journal

Daily Reflection

FAITH-FILLED Rooms

How has your FAITH changed the atmosphere in the places you have dwelled today?

Fast-Forward FAITH Journal

Daily Reflection

FAITH-FILLED Rooms

How has your FAITH changed the atmosphere in the places you have dwelled today?

Fast-Forward
FAITH Journal

Daily Reflection

FAITH-FILLED Rooms

How has your FAITH changed the atmosphere in the places you have dwelled today?

Fast-Forward
FAITH Journal

Daily Reflection

FAITH-FILLED Rooms

How has your FAITH changed the atmosphere in the places you have dwelled today?

Fast-Forward FAITH Journal

Weekly Reflection

What FAITH-FILLED testimonies have been passed on in your home this week?

...in your workplace?

...in your place of worship?

Fast-Forward
FAITH Journal

Daily Reflection

FAITH-FILLED Rooms

How has your FAITH changed the atmosphere in the places you have dwelled today?

Fast-Forward
FAITH Journal

Daily Reflection

FAITH-FILLED Rooms

How has your FAITH changed the atmosphere in the places you have dwelled today?

Fast-Forward
FAITH Journal

Daily Reflection

FAITH-FILLED Rooms

How has your FAITH changed the atmosphere in the places you have dwelled today?

Fast-Forward FAITH Journal

Daily Reflection

FAITH-FILLED Rooms

How has your FAITH changed the atmosphere in the places you have dwelled today?

Fast-Forward
FAITH Journal

Daily Reflection

FAITH-FILLED Rooms

How has your FAITH changed the atmosphere in the places you have dwelled today?

Fast-Forward
FAITH Journal

Daily Reflection

FAITH-FILLED Rooms

How has your FAITH changed the atmosphere in the places you have dwelled today?

Fast-Forward
FAITH Journal

Daily Reflection

FAITH-FILLED Rooms

How has your FAITH changed the atmosphere in the places you have dwelled today?

Fast-Forward
FAITH Journal

Weekly Reflection

What FAITH-FILLED testimonies have been passed on in your home this week?

____

____

____

____

____

____

...in your workplace?

____

____

____

____

____

____

...in your place of worship?

____

____

____

____

____

____

Fast-Forward FAITH Journal

Daily Reflection

FAITH-FILLED Rooms

How has your FAITH changed the atmosphere in the places you have dwelled today?

Fast-Forward
FAITH Journal

Daily Reflection

FAITH-FILLED Rooms

How has your FAITH changed the atmosphere in the places you have dwelled today?

Fast-Forward
FAITH Journal

Daily Reflection

FAITH-FILLED Rooms

How has your FAITH changed the atmosphere in the places you have dwelled today?

Fast-Forward FAITH Journal

Daily Reflection

FAITH-FILLED Rooms

How has your FAITH changed the atmosphere in the places you have dwelled today?

Fast-Forward
FAITH Journal

Daily Reflection

FAITH-FILLED Rooms

How has your FAITH changed the atmosphere in the places you have dwelled today?

Fast-Forward
FAITH Journal

Daily Reflection

FAITH-FILLED Rooms

How has your FAITH changed the atmosphere in the places you have dwelled today?

Fast-Forward
FAITH Journal

Daily Reflection

FAITH-FILLED Rooms

How has your FAITH changed the atmosphere in the places you have dwelled today?

Fast-Forward FAITH Journal

Weekly Reflection

What FAITH-FILLED testimonies have been passed on in your home this week?

...in your workplace?

...in your place of worship?

Fast-Forward
FAITH Journal

Daily Reflection

FAITH-FILLED Rooms

How has your FAITH changed the atmosphere in the places you have dwelled today?

Fast-Forward FAITH Journal

Daily Reflection

FAITH-FILLED Rooms

How has your FAITH changed the atmosphere in the places you have dwelled today?

Fast-Forward FAITH Journal

Daily Reflection

FAITH-FILLED Rooms

How has your FAITH changed the atmosphere in the places you have dwelled today?

Fast-Forward
FAITH Journal

Daily Reflection

FAITH-FILLED Rooms

How has your FAITH changed the atmosphere in the places you have dwelled today?

Fast-Forward
FAITH Journal

Daily Reflection

FAITH-FILLED Rooms

How has your FAITH changed the atmosphere in the places you have dwelled today?

Fast-Forward
FAITH Journal

Daily Reflection

FAITH-FILLED Rooms

How has your FAITH changed the atmosphere in the places you have dwelled today?

Fast-Forward
FAITH Journal

Daily Reflection

FAITH-FILLED Rooms

How has your FAITH changed the atmosphere in the places you have dwelled today?

Fast-Forward
FAITH Journal

Weekly Reflection

What FAITH-FILLED testimonies have been passed on in your home this week?

...in your workplace?

...in your place of worship?

Fast-Forward FAITH Journal

Daily Reflection

FAITH-FILLED Rooms

How has your FAITH changed the atmosphere in the places you have dwelled today?

Fast-Forward FAITH Journal

Daily Reflection

FAITH-FILLED Rooms

How has your FAITH changed the atmosphere in the places you have dwelled today?

Fast-Forward
FAITH Journal

Daily Reflection

FAITH-FILLED Rooms

How has your FAITH changed the atmosphere in the places you have dwelled today?

Fast-Forward
FAITH Journal

Daily Reflection

FAITH-FILLED Rooms

How has your FAITH changed the atmosphere in the places you have dwelled today?

Fast-Forward
FAITH Journal

Daily Reflection

FAITH-FILLED Rooms

How has your FAITH changed the atmosphere in the places you have dwelled today?

Fast-Forward
FAITH Journal

Daily Reflection

FAITH-FILLED Rooms

How has your FAITH changed the atmosphere in the places you have dwelled today?

Fast-Forward
FAITH Journal

Daily Reflection

FAITH-FILLED Rooms

How has your FAITH changed the atmosphere in the places you have dwelled today?

Fast-Forward
FAITH Journal

Weekly Reflection

What FAITH-FILLED testimonies have been passed on in your home this week?

...in your workplace?

...in your place of worship?

A Parting Note...

Friends, I would like to share with you
one last bit of
Vital FAITH counsel
from God's Word:

Above all, taking the shield of faith,
wherewith ye shall be able to quench all the
fiery darts of the wicked.
Ephesians 6: 16

Keep moving at the speed of FAITH!

All Glory be to God!

About the Author

Peggie M. Hall is convinced that God has blessed her with a special anointing to write poetry. She has been writing poetry for the past thirty-three years. Peggie has made sharing her gift with others a personal commitment.

Peggie was born in Aberdeen, Mississippi. She now resides in Saginaw, Michigan with her husband, Gary. She is the blessed mother of two beautiful daughters, Ramona and Tifani, son-in-law, Toriano, Sr., and a very special grandson, Toriano, Jr.

Peggie is a born-again believer and currently serves as a member of Bethel A.M.E. Church, where her Pastor and 1st Lady are P. David and Catherine Saunders. Peggie is an Intercessor, Sunday School Teacher, Mentor, Member of the Christian Education Board, and a Member of the Courtesy Committee.

Peggie is the author of four previous books of poetry. Titles include: *Cutting Down Mountains, A Place Called Peace, Hide It In Your Heart,* and *Sunday Morning On My Mind.*

Printed in the United States
65762LVS00004B/211-288

9 781892 398024